Time-Savers for Teachers

WRITING FICTION YEARS 5-6

W
TTS

How to use this book

This book provides a range of worksheets suitable for children in Years 5 and 6 of primary school. The worksheets are grouped into sections which correspond to the text types specified in the National Literacy Strategy. The contents are equally relevant to the Scottish 5-14 Guidelines, and the curricula for the Republic and Northern Ireland.

Each section starts with an introduction. As well as introducing the worksheets, this also details the National Literacy Strategy objectives and suggests approaches to writing. The worksheets have been carefully selected to cater for *different* levels of ability.

At the end of the section, text frames and scaffolds provide guidance for *creative writing* assignments. There are also *assessment sheets* to enable you to keep track of individual children's progress. All teacher-pages have a vertical stripe down the side of the page.

All the worksheets in this book are photocopiable.

This edition first published in 2004

Franklin Watts
96 Leonard Street, London EC2A 4XD

Contributors: John Barwick, Sharon Dalgleish, Tanya Dalgleish, Karen Dobbie, Ann Doherty, Michael Faye, Angela Lloyd, Sharon Shapiro

UK adaptation by Brenda Stones
Educational advisers: Sarah St John, Jo Owston

This edition not for sale outside the United Kingdom and Eire

ISBN 0 7496 5806 1

Printed in Dubai

Contents

NLS Framework

Year 5

	TERM 1	**TERM 2**	**TERM 3**
Fiction and poetry	•novels, stories and poems by significant children's writers •playscripts •concrete poetry	•traditional stories, myths, legends, fables from a range of cultures •longer classic poetry, including narrative poetry	•novels, stories and poems from a variety of cultures and traditions •choral and performance poetry

Year 6

	TERM 1	**TERM 2**	**TERM 3**
Fiction and poetry	•classic fiction, poetry and drama by long-established authors including, where appropriate, study of a Shakespeare play •adaptations of classics on film/TV	•longer established stories and novels selected from more than one genre, e.g. mystery, humour, sci-fi, historical, fantasy worlds etc. •range of poetic forms, e.g. kennings, limericks, riddles, cinquain, tanka, poems written in other forms (as adverts, letter, diary entries, conversations), free verse, nonsense verse	•comparison of work by significant children's author(s) and poets: (a) by same author (b) different authors' treatment of same theme(s)

Text type grid

Genre	Text	Text type	Year/Term
Poetry	Epistle to the Olympians	Significant children's writer	Y5T1
	Shopping Trolleys	Narrative poem	Y5T2
	Seven Day Cycle	Performance poem	Y5T3
	Death of a Whale	Sonnet	Y6T2
	The Killer / The Crimson Serpent	Comparison of theme	Y6T3
Drama	Fancy's Bell	Playscript	Y5T1
	All hail, Macbeth	Study of a Shakespeare play	Y6T1
Stories	Grinny	Significant children's writer	Y5T1
	The Girl With No Name	Other culture	Y5T3
	The Burnt Stick	Other culture	Y5T3
	Little By Little	Autobiography	Y6T2
	Space Demons	Science fiction	Y6T2

Introduction to Epistle to the Olympians

Level: Year 5 Term 1

Text type: Poem by significant children's writer

NLS objectives:

Y5T1 T6: to read a number of poems by significant poets and identify what is distinctive about the style or content of their poems;

Y5T1 T16: to convey feelings, reflections or moods in a poem through the careful choice of words or phrases.

The text:

Things to talk about:

Explain the title: Epistle is a letter; Olympians, judging from the illustration and the first line, are the parents, i.e. the big Greek gods.

Read the poem aloud to the class.

What feeling is the child expressing? Why did the child choose to write the letter?

Are there any words that are difficult to understand, e.g. kindle, dwindle, rajah, chidings, dunce? Is the language overall formal or informal?

What is the form of the poem? How many lines per verse? What is the rhyme scheme? How many syllables per line?

The worksheets:

Start with discussion of the poem in groups, following the prompt questions on the first sheet. Does the class agree that the child is a girl? The next sheet studies the form and message of the poem in more depth, before the 'st sheet invites a reply letter, preferably following the model of the original quatrain.

Epistle to the Olympians

Dear parents, I write you this letter
Because I thought I'd better;
Because I would like to know
Exactly which way to grow.

My milk I will leave undrunk
If you'd rather have me shrunk,
If your love it will further kindle,
I'll do my best to dwindle;

Or, on the other hand,
do you wish me to expand?
I'll stuff like a greedy rajah
If you really want me larger.

All that I ask of you
Is to tell me which to do;
To whisper in accents mild
The proper size for a child.

I get so very confused
By the chidings commonly used.
Am I really such a dunce
As to err two ways at once?

When one mood you are in,
My bigness is a sin:
"Oh what a silly thing to do
For a big girl like you!"

But then another time
smallness is my crime:
"Stop doing whatever you're at;
You're far too little for that!"

Kind parents, be so kind
As to kindly make up your mind
and whisper in accents mild
The proper size for a child.

by Ogden Nash
from *Custard and Company* (Puffin)

WHEN ARE YOU GOING TO
GROW UP !!

7

Let's talk about it!

Name _____

IF YOU ASK ME, THE CHILD'S NOT CONFUSED...
...BUT THE PARENTS ARE!

Talk with a group about the relationship between the child and her parents that Ogden Nash presents in the poem. Talk about why you think the child is so confused. Write your explanation on the lines below.

_____

_____

_____

Talk about the situations that the child might be referring to in the third last and the second to last stanzas. What things might she be too small to do? What things might she be too big to do? Write your ideas on the lines below.

_____

_____

_____

Think about your parents. What image do you have of them? Talk about it with a partner. Are they like gods? Why, or why not? Which of the ancient Greek gods is most like your mother? Which is like your father? Write an explanation for your choice.

My father is most like:

_____

_____

_____

MY PARENTS **MUST** BE GODS — BECAUSE I'M A PERFECT ANGEL

My mother is most like:

_____

_____

_____

8

Quatrains

Name _____

The four-line stanzas, with their rhyming lines, help to make the poem funny. Talk with a group about the effect of some of the rhymes on your view of the parents, the child and the situation. Write your ideas in the space below.

_____

_____

_____

_____

Look closely at the last stanza. Notice the repetition of the word 'kind'. Talk with a group about this word. Does it mean exactly the same thing each time? Why do you think that the poet has repeated the word? Write your ideas in the space below.

IT TAKES ALL KINDS, BUT YOU CAN NEVER BE TOO KIND.

_____

_____

_____

_____

Is this serious?

An epistle is usually a formal letter with a serious message. The message is generally one that points out a moral position. It tells the reader about correct behaviour. An epistle is usually written by an adult who is in a position of authority or who is held in high esteem in the community.

IF AN EPISTLE IS SO SERIOUS, WHY DOES IT HAVE SUCH A SILLY NAME?

The epistle in this poem is really a send-up. It has a message, but it is quite light-hearted. Talk with a group about your first impressions of the message in this epistle. Write your ideas in the space below.

_____

_____

_____

_____

Write your own epistle

Name _____

Imagine that you are one of the parents of this child. What message has the epistle sent to you? How do you feel about this message? How would you respond to the epistle? Talk about these reactions with a group.

Now write an epistle in response to this one. You may also wish to write your epistle as a send-up. Do your rough work on scrap paper and then write your finished version in the space below.

_____

_____

_____

_____

_____

_____

_____

_____

_____

_____

_____

_____

_____

_____

_____

_____

_____

Introduction to Shopping Trolleys

Level: Year 5 Term 2

Text type: Narrative poem

NLS objectives:

Y5T2 T4: to read a range of narrative poems;

Y5T2 T12: to use the structures of poems read to write extensions based on these, e.g. additional verses, or substituting own words and ideas.

The text:

Read the poem aloud, making sure the class are looking at a copy of the text at the same time. Things to talk about:

What effect does the unusual punctuation and typography have on you?

What kind of creatures are the trolleys compared to? What about the appearance of other inanimate objects, e.g. building-site cranes?

The worksheets:

The first sheet is all about the imagery, or personification, of the trolleys. The second sheet explores the vocabulary, and suggests writing a poem with similar imagery. The last sheet involves a transfer of form, into narrative.

Shopping Trolleys (part 1)

notice how they have perfect steering
until you put something in them

their automatic response is to apply the brakes.
however they can be goaded forward

by the application of a foot sharply placed
on the rear bottom bar. surprise is essential.

you can make them move their wheels
but there is no guarantee that they will all move

in the same direction. the poor things
are terrified & only want to escape. an average

family shopping turns them into nervous
wrecks for weeks. you might think that those

trolleys you see out in car parks & under
sapling trees are sight-seeing. they aren't.

they're trying to avoid having things put in them.
it's hopeless. there's always someone who wants

Shopping Trolleys (part 2)

to use them as garbage bins laundry baskets
billy carts or flower pots. or bassinets.

they are prolific breeders in the wild
& run in enormous herds

they rust in captivity & frequently collapse
during use. recovery is unusual

by Jenny Boult

from *Rattling in the Wind* (Omnibus Books)

Imagery

Name _____

Jenny Boult has created a number of images of shopping trolleys in this poem. Reread the poem and identify some of these images. Write them on the lines below.

_____

_____

Select one image and create a cartoon version of it. You may wish to use some of the words from the poem to label your cartoon.

These trolleys are alive!

Jenny Boult gives the shopping trolleys human or animal qualities. This makes them seem alive, as if they have minds of their own. Reread the poem. List the human and animal qualities that the poet gives to the trolleys. Beside each quality, write words from the poem that indicate it.

_____

_____

_____

_____

_____

_____

14

Playing with words

Name _____

Use a dictionary to find the meaning of the following words, and then explain what these words mean in the context of the poem.

Words	Dictionary meaning	Meaning in poem
automatic		
guarantee		
nervous wrecks		
sapling		
bassinets		
prolific		
captivity		
recovery		

Create your own poem

Write a poem involving an inanimate object. First develop some possible actions and human characteristics for it, then draw the object. Decide whether you will write in first person (as the object) or in third person (as a narrator or through a character). Draft your rough work on scrap paper and write your finished version in the space below.

_____

_____

_____

_____

_____

_____

_____

_____

_____

_____

15

Change the point of view

Name _____

Imagine that you are a supermarket trolley. Think about your life in the supermarket. Write a story about your life. You may wish to draw upon ideas from the poem as well as developing your own view. Draft your story on scrap paper and write the final version in the space below.

> I REMEMBER AS A TWO-YEAR-OLD BASKET GROWING MY FIRST CROOKED WHEELS.

_____

_____

_____

_____

_____

_____

_____

_____

_____

_____

_____

_____

> WANNA DO SOMETHING?

> NO, I WAS OUT ALL LAST NIGHT. THINK I'LL JUST "CRASH".

_____

_____

_____

_____

Introduction to Seven Day Cycle

Level: Year 5 Term 3

Text type: Performance poem

NLS objectives:

Y5T3 T4: to read, rehearse and modify performance of poetry;

Y5T3 T11: to use performance poems as models to write and to produce poetry in polished forms through revising, redrafting and presentation.

The text:

Get seven pupils to perform the poem, taking one verse each.
Things to talk about:

How can they make their movements demonstrate the different mood of each day?

How are the vocabulary and the rhythms used to suggest the different mood of each day?

The worksheets:

The first sheet helps pupils to discuss and analyse the poem in small groups. The next sheet is all about the rhythm and form of the different verses; you may need to check the meaning of ostinato (percussive soundtrack running under spoken words, to reinforce their rhythm), tercet (3-line verses) and stanza (verse). The final sheet suggests using the text as a model for an equivalent poem, in 3-line verses, about the seasons.

Seven Day Cycle

Monday wakes with a wallop,
thrusting into lift off,
launching into the orbit of the week.

Tuesday shakes and shudders,
agitating into action,
driving towards the lunar destination.

Wednesday lolls waylaid in a lull,
coaxing into motion,
easing over the week's hump.

Thursday rouses with a thrumming,
pulling headlong,
pulsing into the rushing stream.

Friday flutters with fiery frenzy,
hurtling down hill,
hurrying to the week's resting place.

Saturday vibrates with its own beat –
a syncopated rhythm
dancing on the grave of the spent week.

Sunday snoozes in somnolent silence –
a supple anacrusis
before Monday's down beat.

by Wendy Michaels

Let's talk about it!

Name _____

Poetry often challenges us to look at the familiar and to see it in a new way. Talk in a small group about why you think poets write this kind of poetry. Share with your group any poems that have made you see familiar things in a new way. Write your group's ideas on the lines.

_____

_____

_____

_____

_____

_____

_____

_____

A life of their own

In this poem, each day seems to have a life of its own because it is described as if it is capable of action. Work with a partner. Identify the action verbs in each stanza. Write these words next to the name of the day. Then write the kind of 'life' that the words attribute to the day. You may wish to ask yourself whether the day seems like something mechanical, human or animal.

Day	Action verb	Kind of life
Monday		
Tuesday		
Wednesday		
Thursday		
Friday		
Saturday		
Sunday		

Get the rhythm

Name _____

The poet identifies a different rhythm for each of the days of the week. Work with a small group. Read the poem aloud. Listen for the rhythm of the words. Develop an ostinato pattern for each of the days of the week. You may want to think about whether this pattern could be made with clicking fingers, tapping on a table, or using percussion instruments. Write the ostinato pattern for each stanza in the space below using a long stroke for a long beat and a short stroke for a short beat. You will need to experiment with how to make the ostinato pattern speed up or slow down according to the rhythm of the day in the stanza.

Stanza 1 _____

Stanza 2 _____

Stanza 3 _____

Stanza 4 _____

Stanza 5 _____

Stanza 6 _____

Stanza 7 _____

Tercets

The poet has chosen the tercet as the stanza form. The first five stanzas have a similar structure, but the sixth and seventh have a different pattern in the second and third lines. Talk with a small group about the stanza patterns. How does the meaning and mood change with the changed pattern. Talk about the images of 'syncopated rhythm' and 'supple anacrusis'. Look these words up in a dictionary if you are not certain of their meanings.

On the lines below, explain why the poet has used a different pattern for the last two stanzas.

_____

_____

_____

_____

Be a poet

Name _____

Use this poem as a model for a poem of your own. Your poem should use tercets and be about the seasons – spring, summer, autumn and winter. You can write about them in any order. Use scrap paper to draft your ideas. Begin by deciding on some action verbs that could be applied to each of the seasons. Think about the images that you associate with each of the seasons. Try to develop some metaphors for these images. Work on developing three lines of poetry about each of the seasons. Share your rough drafts with your friends. Write your final season cycle poem in the space below.

_____

_____

_____

_____

_____

_____

_____

_____

_____

_____

_____

_____

_____

_____

_____

Introduction to Death of a Whale

Level: Year 6 Term 2

Text type: Sonnet

NLS objectives:

Y6T2 T5: to analyse how messages, moods, feelings and attitudes are conveyed in poetry;

Y6T2 T6: to read and interpret poems in which meanings are implied or multi-layered; to discuss, interpret challenging poems with others.

The text:

Read the poem aloud to the class. Things to talk about:

What are the four instances of death that are compared?

What does the poet suggest we feel at each of these instances of death?

Study the form of a sonnet. How many lines? What is the rhyme scheme? Compare with, for example, a Shakespeare sonnet.

The worksheets:

As usual, you start with discussion in small groups. Then the storyboard breaks down the narrative of the part of the poem that describes the whale. On the third sheet, the evocative effects of the vocabulary are explored. Finally pupils write their own poem, and you could apply differentiation as to who could tackle the sonnet form.

Death of a Whale

When the mouse died, there was a sort of pity:
the tiny, delicate creature made for grief.
Yesterday, instead, the dead whale on the reef
drew an excited multitude to the jetty.
How must a whale die to wring a tear?
Lugubrious death of a whale: the big
feast for the gulls and sharks; the tug
of the tide simulating life still there,
until the air, polluted, swings this way
like a door ajar from a slaughterhouse.
Pooh! pooh! spare us, give us the death of a mouse
by its tiny hole; not this in our lovely bay.
– Sorry, we are, too, when a child dies;
but at the immolation of a race, who cries?

by John Blight from *Pattern and Voice* compiled by
John and Dorothy Colmer (Macmillan Australia)

Personal response

Name _____

When we reread poems we often see another level of meaning, or a different viewpoint, from the one we saw in an earlier reading. Reread this poem. Read it aloud listening to the sounds, and silently hearing the echoes. Why has the poet used this particular rhyming scheme? What effect does it have? Write in the space below the ideas that you think the poet is communicating and how he feels about these ideas.

_____

_____

_____

_____

_____

Let's talk about it!

Talk with a partner about the following questions. Write your conclusions on the lines. Why do you think the poet contrasts the size of the whale and the mouse?

_____

_____

_____

The poet also contrasts a child with a race. What do you think the poet is communicating here?

_____

_____

_____

The poet asks the reader two questions. What are these questions? What answer do you think he wants to each question? What answer would you give to each question?

_____

_____

_____

_____

24

Storyboard

Name _____

This poem tells the story of a whale which has beached itself and the effects that this had on the people who came to view it. Create a storyboard for the poem by drawing pictures to match the captions.

1.

The dead whale on the reef drew an excited multitude to the jetty.

2.

The big feast for the gulls and sharks.

3.

The tug of the tide simulating life still there.

4.

The air, polluted, swings this way like a door ajar from a slaughterhouse.

5.

Pooh! pooh! spare us.

6.

Not this in our lovely bay.

Creating a description

_____

In this poem, and from your general reading, you should have
come across noun groups that are used to describe and classify
whales, e.g. large, humpback whale. List these words.

PILOT WHALE

_____

_____

_____

_____

_____

Talk in a group about some of these words and the information that they give about whales.

Word watch

List the words from the poem that you find interesting or unusual. Look up each word in
a dictionary and write its meaning in the table. Talk with a partner about your view of
these words in the poem, and then write how you think the poet has used them.

Word	Dictionary meaning	Meaning in poem

Write your own poem

Name _____

Write your own poem about a whale. You may wish to write a sonnet, using the rhyme pattern that Blight has used. Or, you may prefer to find a different form. Think about the main ideas that you want to communicate to your reader. Try to create clear images that will help you communicate your ideas. You could draw these images first, and then find the words to label the images – creating your poem from these.

Do your first draft on scrap paper and write your finished poem in the space below.

_____

_____

_____

_____

_____

_____

_____

_____

_____

_____

_____

_____

_____

_____

_____

_____

Introduction to The Killer and The Crimson Serpent

Level: Year 6 Term 3

Text type: Different authors' treatment of the same theme

NLS objectives:

Y5T2 W12: to investigate metaphorical expressions and figures of speech from everyday life;

Y6T3 T6: to look at connections and contrasts in the work of different writers.

The texts:

Read the two poems aloud. Things to talk about:

Which snake is real, and which is a metaphor?

How much metaphor is also used in the first poem?

Is the similarity between the two poems just in the subject matter, or also in the language or style?

The worksheets:

The first sheet encourages pupils to discuss their responses, and compare aspects of the two poems. The second encourages debate between different points of view as a vehicle for pupils to work out their deeper responses to the subject matter. Imagery is key to both poems, so the third sheet is dedicated to locating examples of visual and sensory images, and the fourth sheet is devoted to metaphor. Finally, pupils write their own poem, using the kind of imagery and metaphor they have observed in the model texts.

You may wish to introduce or revise these terms before you start: alliteration, assonance, onomatopoeia, metaphor, simile, figurative and emotive language.

The Killer

The day was clear as fire,
the birds sang frail as glass,
when thirsty I came to the creek
and fell by its side in the grass.

My breast on the bright moss
and shower-embroidered weeds,
my lips to the live water
I saw him turn in the reeds.

Black horror sprang from the dark
in a violent birth,
and through its cloth of grass
I felt the clutch of earth.

O beat him into the ground.
O strike him till he dies –
or else your life itself
drains through those colourless eyes.

I struck again and again.
Slender in black and red
he lies, and his icy glance
turns outward, clear and dead.

But nimble my enemy
as water is, or wind.
He has slipped from his death aside
And vanished into my mind.

He has vanished whence he came,
my nimble enemy;
and the ants came out to the snake
and drank at his shallow eye.

by Judith Wright
from *A Human Pattern: Selected Poems*
(ETT Imprint)

The Crimson Serpent

Fire; a serpent, hissing and crackling
Now pacified, now demanding
Climbing and swirling through countless
grotesque form –
Hungrily eyeing the next morsel of food
in its path to self-destruction.
Fire now secluded, now rampant through
the charred ruins of its meal
Now friendly and warm, the next moment
fierce and hot
Desperately trying to escape an inescapable fate –
A crimson serpent with an insatiable appetite,
Doomed to death through its own greediness.

by Charles Cook

Personal response

Talk about both poems with a partner. Then write about how you reacted to each of the poems. This response may describe feelings, thoughts or the approach of the poets.

The Killer

_____

_____

_____

_____

The Crimson Serpent

_____

_____

_____

_____

The snake's image

Compare the way the snake is portrayed in both poems.

	The Crimson Serpent	The Killer
Mood of title		
Setting		
Action verbs		
Noun groups /adjectives		
Tense		

Debate

Name _____

In 'The Killer', the poet's fear leads to the snake's unprovoked and violent death.
Write the speech for the affirmative (positive) or negative argument in a debate of the topic:
Should superstitions be allowed to control our lives? Remember to greet listeners, argue against the
other team's points, write points to support your case and end by thanking people for listening.

_____
_____
_____
_____
_____
_____
_____
_____
_____
_____
_____
_____
_____
_____
_____
_____
_____
_____
_____
_____
_____

Creating images

Name _____

Visual and sensory images are created using figurative language. Find examples of the following in 'The Crimson Serpent'.

Alliteration

_____

_____

Onomatopoeia

_____

_____

Metaphor

_____

_____

Contrasted images

_____

_____

Emotive language

_____

_____

Implied or stated

In poetry, many facts are not clearly explained. Even if a concept or idea is not exactly stated, we can 'read between the lines' to what is implied. With a partner, talk about the ideas in 'The Killer'. Are they implied or stated? Summarise your discussion on the lines below. Hint: you could discuss the setting, the weather and the perception of the snake.

_____

_____

_____

_____

_____

Extended metaphors

Name _____

Different kinds of metaphors or comparisons can be sustained in a poem. Think about what topics could be used as the basis for an extended metaphor poem. You could start by thinking about what your world or school resembles or how the illogical, irrational way you or your friends behave can be compared to the animal or animals inside. Brainstorm your ideas here. Then choose one idea and write the poem.

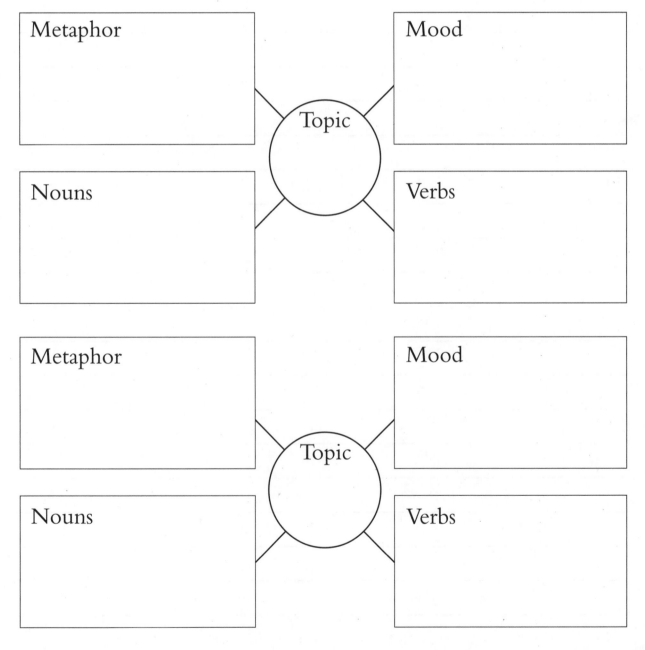

Metaphor

Mood

Topic

Nouns

Verbs

Metaphor

Mood

Topic

Nouns

Verbs

Create a poem

Name _____

Choose a free or captive animal and picture it in your mind's eye. Write phrases describing the animal's colour, shape, movement and contrasts of mood, such as playful, hunting, hungry. Does it have any features peculiar to its species? Is it playful, savage, swift, slow, strong, graceful or intelligent? How will you convey the uniqueness of the animal? Consider adding similes and metaphors. Draft a poem on rough paper and write the final version below.

_____

_____

_____

_____

_____

_____

_____

_____

_____

_____

_____

_____

_____

_____

_____

_____

_____

_____

Poetry writing interview

Name _____

Self-assessment e.g. What type of poetry do you enjoy writing or reading? Is there anything you don't like writing about or find difficult about writing poetry? How do you rate yourself as a poet? Does the shape of the poem contribute to the meaning? What is the purpose of the poem?

Range and preferences e.g. What do you like writing poetry about and for what type of audiences? What strategies do you use to make your poetry clear and interesting? What is the tone of the poem?

Skills e.g. Are your ideas more important than accurate spelling and correct sentence structure? How does the rhythm reinforce and create the meaning of the poem? If the poem rhymes, does it sound natural or contrived? Do word chains built through synonyms, antonyms and repetition appear? Does the poem create sensory images? Does the imagination in the poem help you see things in a new way? Do noun groups, adverbs and adverbial phrases appear in the poem?

Current projects e.g. What poetry are you writing now? What would you like to write?

Poetry skills checklist

Name:				
Class:	Date/Level	Date/Level	Date/Level	Date/Level
PURPOSE				
Understands the purpose of poetry.				
STRUCTURE				
Writes a well-developed series of events when appropriate.				
Able to tie up ends in a clear resolution.				
Varies the stages of a poem when writing, using different structures.				
Recognises different forms of poetry.				
TEXT ORGANISATION				
Develops a well-sequenced plan for poetry writing.				
Uses stanzas appropriately.				
Changes rhythm to indicate a new element or different mood in the poem.				
Able to sequence thoughts clearly.				
Varies the point of view using different perspectives within a poem.				
LANGUAGE FEATURES				
Uses noun groups to create clear images.				
Uses adjectives to identify characters and to write vivid images.				
Uses verbs.				
Uses adverbs and adverbial phrases to indicate, where, when, how.				
Uses word chains built from synonyms, antonyms and repetition.				
Uses first or third person and addresses audience directly, as 'you', at times.				
Uses sensory images for feelings and emotions.				
Uses rhythm appropriate to subject matter.				
Able to rhyme when appropriate.				
Makes use of figurative language.				
Generally begins each line with a capital letter.				
LEVEL CODES	1 Consistently evident		2 Sometimes evident.	3 Not evident

Poetry writing assessment

Name _____

Task e.g. Rhyming, sensory or descriptive poetry; a ballad; a sonnet
Context e.g. Individual, pairs, group, teacher directed

ANALYSIS

Content e.g. Purpose, organisation of verses or format, awareness of audience
Skills e.g. Planning, drafting, editing, redrafting, spelling, punctuation, handwriting
Language study e.g. Appropriate sensory and descriptive language, word chains, noun groups, adverbs and adverbial phrases, action verbs, metaphors for images
Teaching needs e.g. Attitude to task, teaching needed for further development

Drama texts

Structure and features of drama texts

PURPOSE

Drama acts as an avenue to narrate events, to entertain, to create, to emotionally move and to explore the human condition. A play will also socialise, persuade and inform by teaching. Plays are part of an oral storytelling tradition. Any event, real or imagined, can become the topic for the playwright's purpose.

Drama enables students for a period of time to take on another person's perspective and character as they explore important issues, situations, relationships and beliefs. These roles may be similar or different from their own lives. The overall purpose would be to bring about a change in the level of a student's understanding, social behaviour and expectation, and a greater awareness of the needs of others.

STRUCTURE OF DRAMA TEXTS

In a play, the protagonist, the hero who provides the point of view, usually undertakes a dramatic journey or experience that is played to the audience. The conflict is generally created by an antagonist, or something in the environment which upsets the normal way of life.

In a dramatic script we learn about the actors' roles from what they do, what they wear and what they look like. Their strengths and weaknesses become apparent through the dialogue when we hear what they say and what others say about them. In a radio play there are no costumes or scenery to create the time, atmosphere or setting. The script is totally reliant on the narrator's ability to keep the story together (if there is a narrator), the actors' dialogue and sound effects.

Non-naturalistic plays, for example *Fancy's Bell*, do not have a narrative structure holding them together but consist of a series of acts or images that have different characters and different settings. The emphasis is on the characters and their words, music and sound cues.

Most dramatic scripts have the following structure:
– Setting the scene; listing of characters; backdrop; lighting
– Prologue (optional)
– Orientation
– Complication
– Series of events
– Resolution
– Epilogue/Re-orientation (optional)

Setting of the scene

The playwright writes stage directions for the actors to clarify how they should portray their character's actions and movements and, where necessary, how they should speak their lines. Details of the costumes and sound effects are specified.

Prologue

This is an optional way of introducing the setting and the characters. Some background information can be given about the characters, time, setting or even theme of the play. The narrator often relates this information to the audience.

Orientation

This briefly sets the context that can be visualised by the lighting, set, costumes, music and dialogue that creates the atmosphere. The orientation generally comes at the beginning of the play or in the form of a prologue. There must be a character and setting in every story but the conflict is all-important.

Complication

Generally a problem occurs in the character's personal life or with the world in which he or she interacts. The conflict, which must be dramatic and easily understood by the audience, forms the pivotal point of the play.

Series of events

Each act revolves around a complicated series of events that move the dramatic plot along to the point of climax, the most exciting part of the play.

Resolution

This solution to the conflict is generally found in the last act.

Epilogue/Re-orientation

This sets the scene again and relocates the characters. This generally takes place at the end of the play and may take the form of an epilogue.

LANGUAGE FEATURES OF DRAMA TEXTS

- Characterisation is developed through events and dialogue.
- Action verbs are used effectively e.g. walking.
- Evaluative language is found e.g. sad, happy, a look of death, bossy.
- As the audience is present there is no lengthy narrative description as might be found in a story or novel.
- The language may be emotive, realistic, poetic or whatever is necessary for the author's purpose.
- Names of the characters are written before their dialogue so no inverted commas are used for speech. Each character's dialogue begins on a new line.
- Consistent use of first or third person to narrate the script.
- Use of emotive language, often speaking directly to you, the audience.
- Atmosphere is developed through the use of noun groups.
- Adverbs and adverbial phrases tell how, when and where.
- May have a narrator who speaks directly to the audience.
- Effective images used in the dialogue so creates vivid pictures.
- Dialogue in present tense, but narration in the past tense.

Introduction to Fancy's Bell

Level: Year 5 Term 1   **Text type**: Playscript

NLS objectives:

Y5T1 T5: to understand dramatic conventions including:

- the conventions of scripting (e.g. stage directions, asides);

- how character can be communicated in words and gesture;

- how tension can be built up through pace, silences and delivery.

Y5T1 T19: to annotate a section of a playscript as a preparation for performance, taking into account pace, movement, gesture and delivery of lines and the needs of the audience.

The text:

You will need a cast of 12: the girl and boy as they progress through different stages of life. Things to talk about:

Explain the term 'alter ego': the other self, meaning the inner voice of the characters.

Explain at some point the origin of the two songs: the Old Man's from Shakespeare's *Twelfth Night*, and the Old Woman's from Shakespeare's *Merchant of Venice*. Why do you think the playwright chose to quote from them?

You don't necessarily need any staging for the play: it's a stylised sequence of dialogues between the same two characters.

The worksheets:

The first sheet following the script is an example of how to annotate a playscript, as recommended in the NLS objective above; in this case it's annotated more for language features than for performance, but it shows the advantage of being able to copy a page of script and add your own marks to draw attention to particular features.

The subsequent sheets involve discussion, response and planning of how you might stage the play more elaborately. There are plenty of opportunities for written work afterwards.

Fancy's Bell (part 1)

*T*here are many different types of play. This play does not have a narrative or story structure. Instead it presents the audience with a series of related images which communicate the main ideas or issues. The script consists of five scenes, each with different characters.

Characters:

Young boy	Young girl	Boy
Boy's alter ego	Girl	Girl's alter ego
Bride	Groom	Husband
Wife	Old man	Old woman

SCENE 1

A school playground. Young Boy and Young Girl make appropriate actions as they speak these lines in the manner of a playground game.

Young boy:	Mr.
Young girl:	**Miss.**
Young boy:	Meet.
Young girl:	**Kiss.**
Young boy:	More.
Young girl:	**Kisses.**
Young boy:	Mr.
Young girl:	**Mrs.**

Short pause

Both:	**Oranges and lemons, say the bells of St Clements.**
Young boy:	You owe me three kisses.
Young girl:	**Say the bells of St Christopher's.**
Young boy:	When will you pay me? Say the bells of Old Bailey.
Young girl:	**Now or never? Say the bells of Westminster.**

SCENE 2

A public place. Boy and Girl with Alter Egos standing behind each. Boy and Girl make actions as Alter Egos speak.

Boy looks at girl. She is not looking. He looks away.

Boy's alter ego:	I wonder if she...

Girl looks at boy. He is not looking. She looks away.

Girl's alter ego:	I wonder if he...

Boy reaches out hand tentatively without looking at girl.

Boy's alter ego:	Will she...?

Girl reaches out hand tentatively without looking at boy.

Girl's alter ego:	Will he...?

Their hands connect as if by magic.

Boy moves towards girl.

Boy's alter ego: I wonder if...

Girl moves towards boy.

Girl's alter ego: I wonder if...

Boy and girl look at each other.

Boy and girl: Would you like to...? *laugh*

SCENE 3

Outside a church. A frozen moment depicting a wedding photograph with bride and groom in typical blissful pose.

Bride: I do.

Groom places ring on Bride's finger.

Groom: **I do.**

Bride places ring on Groom's finger.
Wedding bells ring.

SCENE 4

Husband and Wife on telephone. Each holds a print of the wedding photograph from the previous scene.

Husband: I know I promised I would be home...

Wife: **This was to be our anniversary...**

Husband: I'm sorry.

Wife: **I'm sorry.**

Husband: That's it, then.

Wife: **That's it, then.**

They both hang up. Stand for a moment alone in a freeze position. They look at the photograph, sigh and look at their wedding rings on their hands.

SCENE 5

Old Man and Old Woman sitting in separate chairs. They speak or sing these words directly to the audience.

Old man: When I was a little tiny boy, With a hey ho, the wind and the rain;
A foolish thing was but a toy, For the rain it raineth every day.

Old woman: **Tell me where is fancy bred, In the heart or in the head?**
How begot, how nourished?

Old man: When I came, alas, to wive, With a hey ho, the wind and the rain;
By swaggering could I never thrive, For the rain it raineth every day.

Old woman: **It is engendered in the eyes, With gazing fed; and fancy dies,**
In the cradle where it lies.

Old man: A great while ago the world began
With a hey ho, the wind and the rain;
But that's all one, our play is done,
And we'll strive to please you every day.

Old woman: **Let us all ring fancy's bell. I'll begin it – ding dong bell.**

Old man: Ding dong bell.

Both: **Ding dong bell.**

They look at each other, smile gently and reach out their hands towards each other.

by Wendy Michaels

Sample annotated text

Fancy's Bell

Contains other text types e.g. sets of instructions to actors, directors and designers

Consistent use of present tense.

Characters:

Young boy	Young girl	Boy	Wife
Boy's alter ego	Girl	Girl's alter ego	Old man
Bride	Groom	Husband	Old woman

Non-naturalistic structure. No narrative linking the scenes but a series of related images communicating the main ideas or issues

SCENE 1

A school playground. Young Boy and Young Girl make appropriate actions as they speak these lines in the manner of a playground game.

Young boy:	Mr.
Young girl:	Miss.
Young boy:	Meet.
Young girl:	Kiss ...

Short pause

Both:	Oranges and lemons, say the bells of St Clements.
Young boy:	You owe me three kisses.
Young girl:	Say the bells of St Christopher's.
Young boy:	When will you pay me? Say the bells of Old Bailey.
Young girl:	Now or never? Say the bells of Westminster.

Use of alliteration e.g. bells, Bailey; now, never; fed, fancy; hey, ho; heart, head.

SCENE 2

A public place. Boy and Girl with Alter Egos standing behind each. Boy and Girl make actions as Alter Egos speak.

	Boy looks at girl. She is not looking. He looks away.
Boy's alter ego:	I wonder if she...
	Girl looks at boy. He is not looking. She looks away.
Girl's alter ego:	I wonder if he...
	Boy reaches out hand tentatively without looking at girl.
Boy's alter ego:	Will she...?
	Girl reaches out hand tentatively without looking at boy.
Girl's alter ego:	Will he...?
	Their hands connect as if by magic.
	Boy moves towards girl.
Boy's alter ego:	I wonder if...
	Girl moves towards boy.
Girl's alter ego:	I wonder if...
	Boy and girl look at each other.
Both alter egos:	Would you like to...? laugh

Use of repetition for effect e.g. looks.

Written in first person 'I'.

Action and thinking verbs e.g. kiss, wonder, will, do, meet.

Sound cues establish each scene. Scenes flow through — there are no breaks

SCENE 3

Outside a church. A frozen moment depicting a wedding photograph with bride ...

Bride:	I do.

Groom places ring on Bride's finger.

Groom:	I do.

Bride places ring on Groom's finger. Wedding bells ring.

Each scene changes time, characters and place

SCENE 4

Husband and Wife on telephone. Each holds a print of the wedding photograph ...

Husband:	I know I promised I would be home...
Wife:	This was to be our anniversary...

They both hang up. Stand for a moment alone in a freeze position.

Atmosphere developed through use of noun groups.

SCENE 5

Old Man and Old Woman sitting in separate chairs. They speak or sing these words ...

Old man:	When I was a little tiny boy, With a hey ho, the wind and the rain;
	A foolish thing was but a toy, For the rain it raineth every day.
Old woman:	Tell me where is fancy bred, In the heart or in the head?
	How begot, how nourished? ...
Old man:	A great while ago the world began
	With a hey ho, the wind and the rain;
	But that's all one, our play is done,
	And we'll strive to please you every day.
Old woman:	Let us all ring fancy's bell. I'll begin it – ding dong bell.
Old man:	Ding dong bell.
Both:	Ding dong bell.

They look at each other, smile gently and reach out their hands towards each other.

Other text types – song

Ideas communicated through images e.g. nursery rhymes, Shakespearean plays.

Let's talk about it!

Name _____

Talk with a partner about the idea of fancy. What does it mean to 'fancy' someone or something? What symbols did you notice in the play? Why do you think the playwright used them? Why do you think the playwright used the title *Fancy's Bell* for this play? Write your conclusions.

_____

_____

_____

_____

What should the actors do?

The script instructs the actors as to what they should say and do on the stage in each scene. The instructions about actions are written in italics. For the first scene there are no detailed instructions as there are for the later scenes. Talk with a partner about the appropriate actions for this scene. Then write the instructions for the actors.

Instructions

Scene 1

Young boy:	Mr.
Young girl:	Miss.
Young boy:	Meet.
Young girl:	Kiss.
Young boy:	More.
Young girl:	Kisses.
Young boy:	Mr.
Young girl:	Mrs.

Both:	Oranges and lemons, say the bells of St Clements.
Young boy:	You owe me three kisses.
Young girl:	Say the bells of St Christopher's.
Young boy:	When will you pay me? Say the bells of Old Bailey.
Young girl:	Now or never? Say the bells of Westminster.

What do you think?

Name _____

In Scene 2 the playwright depicts a situation where a boy and girl are trying to indicate their 'fancy' for each other. The playwright uses a device called 'alter ego'. This allows the audience to know what the characters are really thinking, even though they do not express this to each other through words. At the same time the audience sees the way that they are attempting to make contact with each other.

In a group of four, rehearse this scene with the alter egos standing behind the characters speaking the lines. When you have rehearsed the scene present it to other groups in the class. Spend some time discussing the presentations. Which aspects worked best? What ideas were communicated to the audience?

_____

_____

_____

_____

_____

Talk with a partner about the songs that the Old Man and Old Woman sing. They come from two different plays by Shakespeare about the nature of love and fancy. Why do you think the playwright used them to finish this play? What ideas do they communicate to the audience? How do they link the ideas in the rest of the play? What kind of melody would be appropriate for these lines?

_____

_____

_____

_____

With a partner make up a tune for these songs, or use a tune written for any other song you know. Rehearse the songs and present them to others in the class.

The stage is set

Name _____

This play changes location for each scene. Because the scenes are very short, and because the play is not 'naturalistic' or 'realistic', it does not require realistic sets. Imagine that you are the set and costume designer for this play. Reread the script. Think about what you would want the audience to see on the stage in each scene. Sketch in the boxes below the set and costumes for each scene.

Scene 1

Scene 2

Scene 3

Scene 4

Scene 5

Write a poem

Name _____

Working on your own or with a friend write a poem expressing your ideas about the 'Seven Ages of Man', another Shakespearean idea. Complete a draft on scrap paper and write your final version below.

_____

_____

_____

_____

_____

_____

_____

_____

_____

_____

_____

_____

_____

_____

_____

_____

_____

_____

_____

_____

Introduction to
All hail, Macbeth

Level: Year 6 Term 1

Text type: Study of a Shakespeare play

NLS objectives:

Y6T1 T4: to be familiar with the work of some established authors, to know what is special about their work, and to explain their preferences in terms of authors, styles and themes.

The text:

This is an abridged version of Act I of Shakespeare's *Macbeth*, but the wording is all as in the original.

You need a cast of 5 for these scenes: 3 Witches, Banquo and Macbeth.

Start with the 5 characters reading the script aloud, and practise any of the difficult words they stumble on.

The worksheets:

The sheets move through discussion, to character portrayal, to language analysis, retelling, set design, and prediction. If the class aren't familiar with Shakespeare yet, this is a good way in to a classic scene, and a gentle introduction to period language and dramatisation.

There follows a set of generic sheets on drama writing and assessment, including a sheet on improvisation skills.

All hail, Macbeth (part 1)

Scene 1

Witch 1: When shall we three meet again?
In thunder, lightning and rain?

Witch 2: When the hurly-burly's done,
When the battle's lost and won.

Witch 3: That will be ere the set of sun.

Witch 1: Where the place?

Witch 2: Upon the heath.

Witch 3: There to meet with Macbeth.

All: Fair is foul and foul is fair,
Hover through the fog and filthy
air.

Scene 2

Witch 1: Where has thou been sister?

Witch 2: Killing swine.

Witch 3: Sister, where thou?

Witch 1: A sailor's wife had chestnuts in
her lap,

And muncht, and muncht, and
muncht. 'Give me,' quoth I.

'Aroint thee, Witch' the rump fed
ronyon cries.

ENOUGH WITH THE MACBETH
PREDICTIONS. JUST TELL ME
THE LOTTO NUMBERS.

Her husband's to Aleppo gone,
Master o' th' tiger;

But in a sieve I'll thither sail,

And like a rat without a tail

I'll do, I'll do, and I'll do.

Witch 2: I'll give thee a wind.

Witch 1: Th' art kind.

Witch 3: And I another.

Witch 1: I myself have all the other;
I'll drain him dry as hay;
Sleep shall neither night nor day
Hang upon his pent-house lid;
He shall live a man forbid;
Weary sev'n nights nine
    times nine
Shall he dwindle, peak and pine;
Though his bark cannot be lost,
Yet it shall be tempest-tost.
Look what I have.

Witch 2: Shew me, shew me!

Witch 1: Here I have a pilot's thumb,
Wracked as homeward he did
come.

Witch 3: A drum, a drum; Macbeth doth
come.

All hail, Macbeth (part 2)

All: The weird sisters hand in hand,
Posters of the sea and land,
Thus do go: about, about,
Thrice to thine, and thrice
  to mine,
And thrice again, to make
  up nine.
Peace! the charm's wound up.

Enter Banquo and Macbeth

Macbeth: So foul and fair a day I have not
seen.

Banquo: What are these, so wither'd, and
so wild in their attire?

Macbeth: Speak, if you can: What are you?

Witch 1: All hail, Macbeth, hail to thee,
Thane of Glamis!

Witch 2: All hail, Macbeth, hail to thee,
Thane of Cawdor!

Witch 3: All hail, Macbeth that shalt be
King hereafter!

Banquo: Good sir, why do you start, and
seem to fear
Things that do sound so fair?
To me you speak not.
If you can look into the seeds
  of time,
And say which grain will grow,
  and which will not,
Speak then to me.

Witch 1: Hail!

Witch 2: Hail!

Witch 3: Hail!

Witch 1: Lesser than Macbeth, and greater.

Witch 2: Not so happy, yet much happier.

Witch 3: Thou shalt get kings, though thou
be none.
So all hail, Macbeth and Banquo!

Macbeth: Stay you imperfect speakers, tell
me more!

Witch 1: Banquo and Macbeth! Hail!

Banquo: The earth hath bubbles, as
  water has,
And these are of them. Whither
are they vanish'd?

Macbeth: Into the air; and what
  seem'd corporal
Melted, as breath into the wind.

Banquo: Were such things here as we do
speak about?

Macbeth: Your children shall be kings.

Banquo: You shall be King.

by William Shakespeare
from *Macbeth*

Let's talk about it!

Name _____

Macbeth is a play about ambition and deceit, and our inability to escape our fate. At the time in which Shakespeare wrote, people believed in the power of witches in a way that they do not today. Talk with a group about your view of witches. Write your ideas in the space below.

_____

_____

_____

_____

_____

_____

_____

_____

Create a character profile of a witch. Think of the distinguishing features and select emotive words so you can influence the reader to like or dislike her. Write your character profile on the lines below.

_____

_____

_____

_____

_____

_____

_____

_____

Word watch

Name _____

All the characters in these scenes make reference to opposites. Read the scenes and identify some of these antonyms. Write them in the space below. Then talk with a small group about the ideas that these opposites suggest.

Opposites	What they suggest

Find examples of alliteration, assonance and metaphor in the text.

Alliteration _____

_____

_____

_____

Assonance _____

_____

_____

_____

Metaphor _____

_____

_____

_____

Cartoon action

In these two scenes the witches show how powerful and vengeful they are. Recreate the action of these two scenes in a series of cartoon pictures. Use speech balloons to show what each character is saying in each picture.

Set the scene

Name _____

In the first scene the witches agree to meet 'ere the set of sun'. Imagine that you are the set designer for this scene. Talk with a partner about the stage on which the performance will happen, what the witches will look like, and anything else that will be on the stage. You may want to consider special effects that could be achieved through lighting or sound. In the space below, draw a picture showing the stage with the witches in this scene. Be sure to label your illustration.

What happened next?

Name _____

Think about what might happen to both Macbeth and Banquo in the next part of this play if they meet with the witches again. Would they want to meet separately or together? What might happen in this scene? Talk about it with a partner.

Now write the next scene in which either Macbeth or Banquo meets with the witches. Draft the scene on rough paper and then write the final version in the space below.

_____

_____

_____

_____

_____

_____

_____

_____

_____

_____

_____

_____

_____

_____

_____

_____

_____

From Time-Savers for Teachers: Writing Fiction Years 5-6. This page may be reproduced for classroom use.

55

Drama scaffold

Name

Characters

_____
_____

Scenery and costume suggestions

_____
_____

Prologue
(This is an optional way of introducing the setting and the characters and giving some background information that is important for the play.)

_____
_____

Orientation
(This is generally shorter than in a narrative.)

Who? _____

When? _____

Where?_____

What situation? _____

Why? _____

Complication
(A problem occurs in the character's personal life or in the world around him or her.)

_____
_____

Series of events

_____
_____

Resolution
(The problem in the complication is resolved by one of the main characters.)

_____
_____

Epilogue

_____
_____
_____

Drama writing interview

Name _____

Self-assessment e.g. What ideas do you enjoy writing about in your scripts? Is there anything you don't like writing about or find difficult about writing dramatic scripts? How do you rate yourself as a scriptwriter?

Range and preferences e.g. What do you like writing about and for what type of audiences? What strategies do you use to make your dialogue and action clear and interesting? Do you enjoy mime, improvisation or working from a script? Do you reflect after you have worked on a script to see how you could improve your interpretation?

Skills e.g. How do you plan your stories? How do you edit your work? How do you go about creating interesting and realistic characters? Do you prefer to develop your characters independently or with the support of classmates and your teacher's cues? Are your ideas more important than accurate spelling and correct sentence structure? How do you check spelling if you are unsure of a word?

Current projects e.g. What dramatic scripts are you writing now? Which parts are you happy with and which do you think need more thought? What would you like to write?

Improvisation and storytelling assessment

Name _____

FEATURES	DATE	COMMENTS
Is the pace of the story varied and does the student use pause effectively to build up tension?		
Are the emotions of the story conveyed by the pitch of the voice? How does the pitch of the voice and the intonation suit different characters?		
Does the use of movements, facial expressions and eye contact enhance the story?		
Is sufficient attention paid to how the story begins and how it ends?		
Does an expressive voice effectively convey the mood of the story? Can we hear the anger, happiness, moodiness etc. that the character is feeling?		
Is the storyline conveyed in a sequenced, effective and easy to follow manner?		
Is the student able to take on the role of the character and maintain this in a believable way?		
Is the student confident and able to gain the attention of the audience?		

FOLLOW-UP SUGGESTIONS

Drama skills checklist

Name:				
Class:	Date/Level	Date/Level	Date/Level	Date/Level
PURPOSE				
Demonstrates understanding of the purpose of dramatic scripts.				
STRUCTURE				
Writes a prologue where the scene and background are described.				
Lists characters and costumes, and describes scenery effectively (not for radio scripts).				
Writes a clear but shortened orientation.				
Creates a complication based on an unexpected event.				
Writes a well-developed series of events.				
Able to resolve the situation clearly.				
Able to recognise different types of dramatic scripts.				
TEXT ORGANISATION				
Develops a well-sequenced plan for script writing.				
Able to write a clear sequence of events.				
Writes a resolution connected to the orientation and complication.				
Writes a prologue effectively, tying up any incomplete threads.				
LANGUAGE FEATURES				
Characterisation is developed through dialogue and events.				
Action verbs are used effectively.				
Uses evaluative language.				
Atmosphere is developed through use of noun groups.				
Uses adverbs and adverbial phrases to indicate how, when and where.				
Able to use first or third person consistently.				
Consistently uses correct tense.				
Uses emotive language when speaking to the audience.				
LEVEL CODES	1 Consistently evident	2 Sometimes evident	3 Not evident	

Introduction to Grinny

Level: Year 5 Term 1

Text type: Story by significant children's writer

NLS objectives:

Y5T1 T10: to evaluate a book by referring to details and examples in the text;

Y5T1 T15: to write new scenes or characters into a story, in the manner of the writer, maintaining consistency of character and style, using paragraphs to organise and develop detail.

The text:

Things to talk about:

Have the class read any other books by Nicholas Fisk? He is known for science-fiction stories, like this one.

How does the layout of the text lead you into the story? Newspapers often use this technique.

Read the extract aloud and ask how the class respond; does it make them want to read the rest of the book?

The characters are actually a brother and sister talking about their aunt, Great Aunt Emma.

The worksheets:

The follow-up sheets concentrate on the genre of science fiction, and the description and development of the characters. There is plenty of opportunity for extended writing, including a sheet on reviewing a book of their choice.

Grinny

I said, 'Oh.' I was disappointed in her for being so childish, actually.

She said, 'Yes, I knew you would take it like that, you just think I'm stupid, but I'm not. Grinny is not real, she's not a real person at all.'

It went on like this for a little while, then I said, 'Tell me exactly and precisely what you are talking about and no messing about and above all do not cry.'

She said, 'You remember the day she fell down on the ice and hurt herself?' I said yes.

'Well, I was the first one there, I was there just about a second after she did it, she was still lying on the ground and I was there beside her. And I saw something you'll never believe, never!'

I said what was it and I would try to believe her.

She said, 'Something horrible, it was horrible! I saw her wrist actually broken and the bones sticking out!'

I replied, 'That's impossible. Do be reasonable, she was perfectly alright quite soon after. If you break your wrist it is very serious, it takes weeks or months to mend. Particularly if you are old. And it is very painful, agony, in fact. So you just couldn't have seen it, Beth, you only thought you saw it because you have a good imagination.'

Beth said, 'I haven't got a good imagination. Penny writes much better essays than I do and so does Sue. I saw it, I saw it, I saw it!'

So I made her tell me just what it was she saw. She started off by repeating that I would never believe her and so on, but in the end it came down to this – I am choosing my words very carefully so as not to distort what she said –

'She was lying on the ground in a heap. She was not groaning or moaning, just lying there kicking her legs, trying to get up. I went close to her and got hold of her elbow so that I could help pull her up. She did not say anything to me, like "Help me" or "My wrist hurts" – she just tried to get up. When I seized her elbow I saw her wrist. The hand was dangling. The wrist was so badly broken that the skin was all cut open in a gash and the bones were showing.'

I told Beth I understood all this but she seemed unwilling to go on. She looked at me and wailed 'Oh it's no good, you'll never believe me!' But I made her go on. She said:

'The skin was gashed open but there was no blood. The bones stuck out but they were not made of real bone – they were made of shiny steel!'

by Nicholas Fisk
from *Grinny* (William Heinemann, a division of Egmont Children's Books Limited)

What's so unusual about Grinny breaking her wrist?

It was the bones!

What do you think?

Name _____

Does the extract make you want to read the whole book? Why or why not? Give reasons for your opinion.

_____

_____

_____

_____

_____

_____

_____

Who is Grinny?

The character 'Grinny' in the extract is Tim and Beth's Great Aunt Emma. Draw a picture of what you imagine her to look like. Include labels in your drawing.

Character description

Name _____

In narrative texts, verbs convey what characters are thinking, saying and feeling. These help us empathise with characters. Pick out the different kinds of verbs and write them below.

Thinking or feeling verbs	Doing or action verbs	Saying or asking verbs

Consider the verbs used by different characters in the extract e.g. was disappointed. Choose a character and describe how you see them.

_____

_____

_____

_____

_____

_____

What happens next?

Name _____

The extract is part of a conversation between the narrator, Tim, and his sister Beth.
What do you think might happen next? Write the next section of the narrative. Write
in first person in the role of Tim, and try to maintain the same style of writing.
Draft on scrap paper and then write your final version on the lines below.
If necessary, attach more paper.

_____

_____

_____

_____

_____

_____

_____

_____

_____

_____

_____

_____

_____

_____

_____

_____

Your turn

Name _____

Write a science-fiction narrative. Decide what kind of science fiction it will be (for example, time travel, aliens, space travel etc.). You will probably need to do some research so that you can use accurate terminology to make your narrative convincing and credible. Remember to take into account the structure of a narrative text and the importance of thinking and feeling verbs for engaging readers' interest and empathy.

Plan your narrative on the lines below, draft it on scrap paper and then write your final version on another sheet.

_____

_____

_____

_____

_____

_____

_____

_____

_____

_____

_____

ZIBBY DIBBY
NABBER DAB

_____

_____

_____

_____

_____

65

Review raves

Name _____

When you have finished reading your chosen novel, write a review of it. The review should start with a description of the type of work, explanation of the setting and a brief summary of the text. This should be followed by a description of the main character and their relationships. Finally, state your opinions or make a judgement evaluating the text. After editing a draft copy of the review, write your final version on the lines below.

_____

_____

_____

_____

_____

_____

_____

_____

_____

_____

_____

_____

_____

_____

_____

_____

_____

_____

Introduction to The Girl With No Name

Level: Year 5 Term 3

Text type: Story from another culture

NLS objectives:

Y5T3 T1: to investigate a range of texts from different cultures, considering patterns of relationships, social customs, attitudes and beliefs:

- identify these features by reference to the text;

- consider and evaluate these features in relation to their own experience.

Y5T3 T2: to identify the point of view from which a story is told and how this affects the reader's response.

The text:

Things to talk about:

What clues do the name and the illustration give about the cultures involved here? The story is about an Aboriginal community.

Read the story aloud, and invite discussion about Matthew's perception of the family and the community.

What does the grandmother's answer indicate about the Aboriginal sense of identity?

The worksheets:

The first sheet invites discussion, and then a plan of the structure of the story. The following sheets investigate place and then character. Finally, the issue of large and small families is picked up on, for preparing a debate from different points of view.

The Girl With No Name

Matthew had no idea what Napangarti meant, but he knew the old woman must be talking about her granddaughter. 'Oh dear.' He was crestfallen, wondering why her brother hadn't told him that. 'Do you know where she is?'

The old woman shook her head, but said nothing. Matthew wanted to question her further, but didn't like to do so in case she thought him rude.

He looked around, trying not to make his curiosity too obvious. The houses were all the same design, single storey, built flat on the ground, with only the colouring to distinguish them. They had been arranged in an oval, with a road running around the front of them. In the central space created by the arrangement of the houses, which was evidently intended to be a sort of park, stood one or two biggish old eucalyptus trees, but there was no grass. The ground was bare and dusty and marked with innumerable tyre tracks. A few front yards sprouted patches of grass and in some of them young trees were growing, but most were of bare earth like the central space.

There were no fences between the houses, and Matthew sensed that the people here lived much more closely and publicly than his own kind did. He remembered the community name at the entrance. This did indeed look like a community. He thought it might be alright to live like that, amongst other families instead of walled-up behind a fence as his family was, intent on privacy. But then he thought of his neighbours. He couldn't imagine wanting to be seen by them whenever he moved out of his house. Perhaps it was necessary to know people very well before you could feel comfortable living this closely with them.

Matthew was used to being an only child and had never worried about it, but now he was struck by the thought that he could be missing out by having no relations living nearby besides his parents. He felt a touch of envy for No-Name's way of life. She mightn't have much in the way of belongings, but she had her place in the midst of all these people.

No-Name's grandmother didn't seem inclined to give any more information, so after a few minutes Matthew said goodbye to her and wheeled his bicycle out through the entrance.

by Pat Lowe
from *The Girl With No Name* (Puffin)

Let's talk about it!

Name _____

Talk to a partner about the text. Discuss what you think the
book might be about. Write your thoughts on the lines below.
What questions would you like answered about the
characters and events?

IT'S OBVIOUSLY ABOUT
PEOPLE WHO DON'T
HAVE NAMES.

NOT!

_____

_____

_____

_____

_____

Using this extract as an orientation for a story of your own, use the Narrative scaffold
(p. 92) to plan the complication, series of events and resolution. Write the final copy
below. Use more paper if you need to.

_____

_____

_____

_____

_____

_____

_____

_____

_____

_____

_____

_____

_____

Draw a plan

Name _____

Draw a plan of the setting, i.e. the buildings, the park
and the trees, as described in the extract.

Describe a place

Name _____

Describe a place with which you are familiar. Build interesting noun groups, adjectives, adverbs and adverbial phrases, and effective sensory images to write an accurate and detailed description. Draft this on scrap paper and then write your final version on the lines below. Give your description to a partner and have them draw a plan of the place you have described.

_____

_____

_____

_____

_____

_____

_____

_____

_____

_____

_____

_____

_____

_____

_____   SOMETIMES COLD
                                    SOMETIMES HOT   YOUR BATH ?
_____   SOMETIMES FULL
                                    SOMETIMES NOT
_____

_____

_____

_____

Character description

Name _____

Find the verbs in the extract that let the reader know what Matthew is thinking and feeling. Use these to help you write a character profile for Matthew. Remember that every opinion you have of Matthew's character must be supported by evidence in the extract.

_____

_____

_____

_____

_____

_____

_____

_____

_____

_____

_____

_____

_____

_____

_____

_____

_____

_____

Polarised debate

Name _____

Think about the advantages and disadvantages of being a member of a large family and of being a member of a small family. Make notes to prepare for a polarised debate, titled 'Big families are better than small families'.

Advantages: _____

_____

_____

_____

_____

_____

_____

_____

_____

_____

Disadvantages: _____

_____

_____

_____

_____

_____

_____

_____

_____

Introduction to The Burnt Stick

Level: Year 5 Term 3

Text type: Story from another culture

NLS objectives:

Y5T3 T3: to change point of view, e.g. tell incident or describe a situation from the point of view of another character or perspective;

Y5T3 T7: to write from another character's point of view, e.g. re-telling an incident in letter form.

The text:

Read the text aloud. Things to talk about:

Try to list all the times and places in history when an event like this might have happened.

List all the characters, and describe the role and responsibility of each one in the narration.

The worksheets:

The feelings in response to this story are crucial: how disturbed do readers feel at the cruelty and injustice?

Pupils are encouraged to imagine the feelings from the point of view of all the different characters, especially the victim, John.

The Burnt Stick

One night,
when the young moon had risen and they were sitting around the fire, Charlie Warragin, the head stockman, looked at John's mother and said, 'Liyan, I have heard they are coming to take away your son in the morning.'

John Jagamurra felt his mother become very tense, her fear flowing into himself. She held him tighter in her arms and cried, 'Who is coming to take him away? Where will they take him?'

'The Big Man from Welfare,' said Charlie Warragin. 'I have heard he is travelling with the police truck to all the camps in this part of the country, and taking the light-skinned ones to the Fathers at Pearl Bay. He was with the mob at Richmond Downs the day before yesterday. He will be here tomorrow.'

'When will they bring my son back to me?'

'He will not be coming back,' said Charlie Warragin. And the old man, Jabal, who knew much and taught the law to the young men, agreed. 'They will bring him up in the ways of the white man. It will be many years before he can return, but his life will never be the same.'

'They cannot do this thing!' cried Liyan.

'They can, and they will. It is the law of the white man that says so.'

'I will tell the Boss ... tell Mrs Grainger. She will stop them.'

'She will be able to do nothing.'

'I love my son! This is his family! They cannot come to take him away!'

'They have been coming from the day he was born,' said Jabal.

by Anthony Hill
from *The Burnt Stick* (Viking)

What do you feel?

Name _____

How did you feel as you read the extract?
Write your response on the lines below.

_____

_____

_____

_____

_____

_____

Talk with a partner about the text. What do you think it might be about? Discuss
the terms: 'the light-skinned ones', 'the Fathers at Pearl Bay', 'the Big Man from Welfare',
'the mob'. What do you think these terms mean? Write your conclusions
on the lines below.

_____

_____

_____

_____

_____

The 'law' is mentioned twice in the text. What do you think the term means each time?
Talk with a partner and write your answer.

_____

_____

_____

What is meant by: 'They have been coming from the day he was born'?

_____

_____

Point of view

Name _____

Continue this extract, starting from the complication when 'the Big Man from Welfare' arrives to take John away. Imagine that you are John and write in the first person (I). Plan your story carefully, describing the complications, series of events and resolutions, but change the order to suit your storyline. Revise, edit and proofread your draft and write the final version below.

_____

_____

_____

_____

_____

_____

_____

_____

_____

_____

_____

_____

_____

_____

_____

_____

_____

_____

_____

Introduction to Little By Little

Level: Year 6 Term 2

Text type: Autobiography

NLS objectives:

Y6T2 T1: to understand aspects of narrative structure: how authors handle time, e.g. flashbacks, stories within stories, dreams; how the passing of time is conveyed to the reader;

Y6T2 T11: to write own story using, e.g. flashbacks or a story within a story to convey the passing of time.

The text:

Things to talk about:

Consider the difference between biography and autobiography, and some of the issues that would arise if you tried to write an autobiography.

This note was the preface to the author's autobiography; discuss the role of a preface to this kind of text.

Read the text aloud.

What are the issues between fiction and non-fiction raised in the first paragraph?

What are the issues about truthfulness and point of view raised in the second paragraph?

The worksheets:

After the first sheet on discussion and depiction, there is a crucial page on first and third person narratives. Then students are invited to try writing a scene from their own autobiography, bearing in mind what the author said about fact and fiction, and how characters from your life might respond.

Little By Little

When I was a child, I refused to read a 'blue-card book'. The blue cards were in the pockets in the backs of the non-fiction books in the Guelph Public Library. I liked stories better than facts. So as I began telling the story of my life, in spite of myself, it turned into a tale compounded of both truth and imagination. Although everything that happens in these pages has truth in it, not every word is based on fact. I took my memories and rearranged them, filling in details as I went along. I do not really remember every word that I or others said so long ago. I do, however, know exactly how it felt and what we were likely to have said. If I had included all the background material of which I was then ignorant, this might have turned into a full-scale, factual autobiography. I could not let that happen. The child I was would never have forgiven me.

If you find yourself portrayed inaccurately in these pages, remember that memory – yours as well as mine – is a chancy thing and not to be trusted. I have tried to write faithfully of my life as it seemed to me. If you have a different story to tell, go right ahead. I would love to read your version.

by Jean Little
from *Little By Little* (Puffin)

SHE HAS A NICE WAY OF SAYING SHE MADE THE WHOLE THING UP!

Let's talk about it!

Name _____

This extract is from the author's note at the beginning of a book called *Little By Little*. What sort of book do you think it is?

_____

_____

_____

To whom is the author speaking when she issues the invitation, 'If you have a different story to tell, go right ahead'?

_____

_____

_____

Have you ever read a book that someone else hated and you thoroughly enjoyed? Or have you ever seen a movie that bored you senseless yet someone else had recommended it? Write about it.

_____

_____

_____

Depictions

Work with two others in your class to create a depiction. A depiction is a frozen picture, created from your own bodies and some furniture or props, to depict an event. Discuss with the other members of your group what scene you will depict. Ensure that you use body language to communicate tension in your depiction. Show your depiction to others in your class. Write the dialogue best suited to your depiction below.

_____

_____

_____

_____

First and third person

Name _____

The extract is written in the first person. This means that the author uses 'I' to refer to herself throughout the book. Novels are written in either the first person or the third person. In the third person, the author writes about the characters (and from one or more points of view) but is not one of them. Visit your library and find a novel that is written in the first person and one that is written in the third person. Choose a paragraph from each novel to read to a group of classmates. Rehearse your reading.

Record the details of the two books.

	Author	Title	Publisher	Date	Page
first person					
third person					

What's the difference?

Write down some differences you noticed between the novel in the first person and the novel in the third person.

_____

_____

_____

_____

_____

_____

_____

Autobiography

Name _____

Write a scene from your autobiography. Write in the first person. Plan your narrative carefully and draft it after using the Narrative scaffold. Read your writing to a partner and ask for their suggestions. Revise your narrative and then write your final version on the lines below. If you need more room, write on extra paper and attach it to this sheet.

_____

_____

_____

_____

_____

_____

_____

_____

_____

_____

_____

_____

_____

_____

_____

_____

_____

Introduction to Space Demons

Level: Year 6 Term 2

Text type: Science fiction

NLS objectives:

Y6T2 T2: to analyse how individual paragraphs are structured in writing, e.g. comments sequenced to follow the shifting thoughts of a character, examples listed to justify a point and reiterated to give it force;

Y6T2 T10: to use different genres as models to write, e.g. short extracts, sequels, additional episodes, alternative endings, using appropriate conventions, language.

The text:

Read the text aloud. Things to talk about:

Which is the one paragraph that departs from reality? How is that one paragraph constructed, to take us out of the story?

Is any other part of the narrative about science fiction?

The worksheets:

After the personal response, pupils look at character, structure, and terminology particular to the genre, before writing their own science-fiction text.

Then follows a section of generic sheets on writing narrative, that may be of use at any point in the section on stories.

Space Demons (part 1)

At that moment Marjorie called up the stairs, 'Ben, your mother just phoned to say you're to go home now.'

'I can offer to let him play now,' Andrew thought. 'He'll have to say no.'

But Ben did not say no. He could not resist having another shot at Space Demons. Andrew got up grudgingly, and the boys changed places. Ben moved the joystick to guide the spaceman to the gun.

He got it quite quickly. He had been watching Andrew closely and memorising the sequence of the space demons' attack. It was ordered, not random, and it was possible to predict what they were going to do. He was used to computer and video games, he had an inbuilt feel for them, and his hand–eye co-ordination was excellent. So he avoided the space demons, and destroyed them, and kept the

Space Demons (part 2)

little spaceman alive longer and longer, and the score went up and up and up: 30 000, 35 000, 39 000.

'Ben!' Marjorie called again. 'You must go!'

And Ben went. One moment he was sitting in front of the computer screen, totally absorbed in the game; the next he had vanished. Andrew jumped to his feet with a cry of surprise. On the screen the spaceman continued to zap the space demons, twisting, turning and firing, but the chair where Ben had sat was empty, and the joystick did not move.

It only lasted for a moment. The spaceman was shot from behind. The computer gave a sigh and Ben gave a gasp. He was sitting in the chair again. Andrew stared at him, not knowing what to say. Ben's face was white, and he was flexing his right hand as though he had been holding something in it. He turned to look at Andrew and his eyes were dark and wide and amazed.

'That was horrible,' he said. 'I felt as if I was right in the game, as if I was the spaceman, blasting the demons, and then...then I got blasted... .' His voice trailed off. He couldn't put into words the terrifying feeling of black and instantaneous nothingness that came between being shot and finding himself in the chair again. He shivered and then, pulling himself together, forced himself to grin at Andrew. 'Some game!' he said.

by Gillian Rubinstein
from *Space Demons* (Puffin)

What do you think?

Name _____

What do you think of the extract?

_____

_____

_____

_____

_____

_____

_____

Would you like to read the whole book? Why or why not?

_____

_____

_____

_____

Point of view

Whose point of view is represented in the extract? How do you know?

_____

_____

_____

_____

_____

_____

Constructing characters

Name _____

Here is another extract from the book *Space Demons*.

Ben Challis liked and admired Andrew, but Andrew tended to consider Ben as a sort of useful sidekick – he called all the shots and Ben invariably went along with whatever he wanted. As a result, Andrew did not always treat Ben very well.

Construct character profiles for Andrew and Ben. You may wish to construct a web or a list for each character. Base your profiles on the information given in the two extracts.

Andrew's character profile

Ben's character profile

Narrative structure

Narratives typically contain an orientation, complication, series of events and a resolution, though not always in this order. The event described in the extract is one of the series of events involving the characters in the narrative. On the lines below, write an orientation for the narrative.

Remember that an orientation usually places a story in space and time and introduces the main characters.

Remember to include noun groups (nouns and adjectives), clear images, adverbs and adverbial phrases. Plan your orientation on scrap paper first.

_____

_____

_____

_____

_____

_____

_____

_____

_____

_____

_____

_____

_____

_____

_____

_____

_____

_____

Technical terminology

Name _____

Consider the technical terms and scientific jargon in the extract which show that the novel draws on scientific knowledge. Write some of the terms on the lines.

_____

_____

_____

_____

_____

Do you think the author wrote the book for a general audience of readers or for computer buffs? Give reasons for your response.

_____

_____

_____

_____

_____

Consider the following text. It is an extract from an advertisement for a computer. Who do you think is the audience for this advertisement? Where do you think you would find such an advertisement? Write your answer on the lines below.

Technocomp introduces its PCII range of modular notebook PCs with docking capability. The PCII 's modular design covers the CPU kernel (486 DX2–50, DX4–75 or DX4–100). The screen (9.5" mono, 10" Dual Scan colour, 9.5" TFT active matrix colour), the hard disk (200Mb, 340Mb or 510Mb) and the RAM (4, 8, 12 or 20Mb).

_____

_____

_____

_____

_____

Writing challenge

Write a science-fiction narrative. You will probably need to do some research first. You will need to use accurate terminology so that your narrative is convincing and credible. You will need to be able to write expertly about the area of scientific knowledge upon which you are basing your narrative. Write in the third person. Remember to take into account the structure of a narrative text, and the importance of verbs for engaging reader interest and empathy.

Draft your narrative on scrap paper first then write your final version here.

_____

_____

_____

_____

_____

_____

_____

_____

_____

_____

_____

_____

_____

_____

_____

_____

_____

_____

Narrative outline

Name _____

Setting	Main characters

Orientation

Complication

Evaluation

Series of events

Coda/Resolution

Narrative scaffold

Name _____

Orientation
Remember, with more complicated narratives order the stages to suit the storyline.
For example, resolution, complication, evaluation, series of events.

When? _____
_____

Where? _____
_____

Who? _____
_____

What situation? _____
_____

Why? _____
_____

Complication
The order of events or way of life of one of the main characters changes. A problem that eventually must be resolved occurs.

1 _____
2 _____
3 _____

Evaluation
The narrator or one of the main character's comments on what has happened or what may happen next.

_____
_____
_____

Series of events
1 _____
2 _____
3 _____

Resolution
The complications are resolved by one of the main characters.

_____
_____
_____

Re-orientation
(how things are now – optional)

_____
_____
_____

Narrative writing interview

Name _____

Self-assessment e.g. What do you like writing about? Is there anything you don't like writing about or find difficult about writing? How do you rate yourself as a writer? Can you direct your writing to a particular audience? Are you able to write from a particular point of view? Can you vary the point of view from which you narrate within a narrative?

Range and preferences e.g. Have you tried writing autobiographical, science-fiction, fantasy, realistic and historical narratives? What do you like writing about and for what type of audiences? What strategies do you use to make your writing clear and interesting? Do you vary the structure that you use for different effects?

Skills e.g. How do you plan your stories? Do you experiment with different ways of structuring by omitting or beginning with different stages? How do you edit your work? Are your ideas more important than accurate spelling and correct sentence structure? How do you check if you are unsure of spelling?

Current projects e.g. What are you writing now? Which parts are you happy with and which do you think need more thought? Have you varied the structure of your narrative? What would you like to write?

Writing record

Name _____

DATE	TITLE	DRAFT	REDRAFT	TEXT TYPE	THEME	RESPONSE TO WRITING

Narrative skills checklist

Name:				
Class:	Date/Level	Date/Level	Date/Level	Date/Level
PURPOSE				
Understands the purpose of narratives.				
STRUCTURE				
Writes a clear orientation.				
Creates complications based on unexpected events.				
Writes a separate evaluation or as a part of the complication/resolution.				
Writes a well-developed series of events.				
Able to tie up ends in a clear resolution.				
Works with the stages of a narrative to write a more developed and varied structure.				
Recognises different types of narratives.				
TEXT ORGANISATION				
Develops a well-sequenced plan for narrative writing.				
Writes a well-developed, clear orientation.				
Uses paragraphs for new stages or new developments in the complications.				
Able to write a clear sequence of events.				
Writes a resolution connected to the orientation and complication.				
Varies the point of view using different perspectives within a tale.				
Works flexibly within the stages to create a more developed narrative.				
LANGUAGE FEATURES				
Uses noun groups to create clear images in descriptions.				
Uses adjectives to identify characters.				
Uses verbs to indicate thoughts and feelings.				
Uses adverbs and adverbial phrases to indicate where, when, how.				
Uses dialogue correctly to build up interesting narratives.				
Uses first or third person correctly.				
Uses connectives and conjunctions of time to join sentences.				
Uses past tense consistently.				

LEVEL CODES   1 Consistently evident   2 Sometimes evident   3 Not evident

Narrative writing assessment

Name _____

Task e.g. writing an autobiography, science-fiction, fantasy, historical, realistic narrative or stage of a narrative

Context e.g. individual, pairs, group, teacher directed

ANALYSIS

Content e.g. purpose, text organisation, point of view, awareness of audience

Skills e.g. planning, drafting, editing, redrafting, spelling, punctuation, paragraphing, handwriting

Language study e.g. use of nouns, adjectives, adverbs, adverbial phrases, action verbs, dialogue, consistent tenses, conjunctions joining complex sentences

Teaching needs e.g. attitude to tasks, teaching needed for further development